From Passion to Paycheck: Mastering the Creator Economy

Neal Grossheider

Introduction

What is the Creator Economy?
Picture this: You're scrolling through your favorite social media platform, watching a video on how to bake the perfect chocolate cake or maybe catching up on a podcast where your favorite influencer spills all the behind-the-scenes tea. Ever wonder how these creators seem to be living the dream, sharing content they love and actually getting paid for it? Welcome to the **Creator Economy**—where people like you turn their passions into profits by sharing their unique voices, ideas, and talents with the world.

In the simplest terms, the Creator Economy refers to individuals who create digital content—whether it's YouTube videos, Instagram posts, blogs, podcasts, or even online courses—and make a living from it. But we're not just talking about casual posting. This is a booming, multi-billion-dollar industry where creators (aka you!) are shaping the future of media, marketing, and entrepreneurship.

It includes influencers who build huge followings, artists who sell digital prints, vloggers who entertain with daily antics, podcasters who interview inspiring guests, and bloggers who turn words into revenue. The tools of the trade are digital platforms like YouTube, Instagram, TikTok, Patreon, and more, allowing creators to connect with audiences and—here's the cool part—get paid for it!

But it's not just about entertainment or art; it's about turning creativity into a career. Think of it as the new-age version of entrepreneurship. You're not just creating content; you're creating a business around your brand, ideas, and expertise. Whether you're an artist, educator, comedian, fitness guru, or DIY expert, the Creator Economy is where you can share your skills and passion, and get paid while doing it. Sounds like a dream, right?

Purpose of the Book
This book is your no-fluff, straight-to-the-point guide on how to understand, enter, and thrive in the Creator Economy—without all the confusing jargon or intimidating business strategies that feel like they require an MBA. Whether you're a newbie wondering how to get started or a seasoned creator trying to figure out how to scale your income, this book is designed to break down the steps into easy-to-follow, actionable strategies.

Here's what you'll learn:

- How to identify your niche (because yes, the world is waiting for your unique voice!)
- How to build a personal brand that people connect with and trust
- How to make money doing what you love through various income streams like sponsorships, selling your own products, or even starting a membership community
- How to market yourself and grow your audience without feeling overwhelmed by all the platforms and algorithms
- And perhaps most importantly, how to navigate the inevitable bumps in the road (spoiler: criticism, competition, and burnout can happen—but we've got tips for that, too!)

This book will give you the playbook you need to go from creating content as a hobby to turning it into a viable, thriving career. We'll help you cut through the noise, get organized, and start building the life you've dreamed about—one piece of content at a time.

Whether you're dreaming of becoming the next big influencer or you simply want to earn extra income from a side hustle, the Creator

Economy is full of opportunities, and this book is here to help you grab them. Let's dive in and unlock your creative potential together.

Chapter 1: Understanding the Creator Economy

Overview of Trends and Platforms

To truly grasp the magnitude of the Creator Economy, we first need to dive into the platforms where creators make their magic happen. Whether it's bite-sized videos, thought-provoking blogs, or a well-timed meme, creators are making their mark on a variety of digital platforms—each with its own quirks, audiences, and opportunities. Let's explore the heavy hitters.

YouTube:
The OG of the Creator Economy. YouTube is where it all started for many successful creators. With over 2 billion monthly users (yes, *billion*), YouTube offers a massive audience for everything from gaming tutorials to makeup transformations, product reviews to daily vlogs. What makes YouTube stand out is its monetization options. Creators can earn ad revenue, partner with brands, and sell merchandise right from their channels. Plus, with YouTube's algorithm, even small creators can gain traction if they crack the code (spoiler alert: consistency, quality, and catchy thumbnails work wonders).

Instagram:
Instagram is the land of beautifully curated photos, snappy captions, and the almighty *Stories*. While it began as a photo-sharing app, it's now a hub for creators who want to engage visually and connect with their audience in real time. Instagram is also a goldmine for influencers

and brands to collaborate, with sponsored posts, brand partnerships, and the swipe-up link becoming major revenue streams. Creators who can create aesthetically pleasing content while being authentic (yes, even those #nofilter posts) tend to flourish here.

TikTok:
Ah, TikTok—the app that took the world by storm, one 15-second video at a time. It's not just for viral dances and lip-syncs anymore. Creators on TikTok have carved out niches in education, comedy, DIY, and more. With its "For You" page, TikTok's algorithm gives even brand-new creators the chance to go viral with the right mix of creativity and timing. And with over 1 billion active users, it's quickly become one of the hottest platforms for creators to build an audience and connect with brands.

Patreon:
While Instagram, YouTube, and TikTok are all about growing a massive following, Patreon focuses on monetizing that audience. Creators offer exclusive content in exchange for monthly subscriptions from fans, creating a steady income stream. Whether you're a podcaster, artist, writer, or YouTuber, Patreon allows you to offer behind-the-scenes content, early access, or even custom artwork. It's like having your very own fan club that pays you to create.

Key Statistics:

- **YouTube:** 2+ billion monthly active users, with over 1 billion hours of video watched per day.
- **Instagram:** 1.3 billion monthly users, and over 90% of accounts follow a business or creator.
- **TikTok:** 1 billion monthly users, with 41% of users aged 16-24.
- **Patreon:** Over 250,000 active creators, with some earning thousands of dollars a month from their loyal supporters.

What do these stats tell us? The Creator Economy is thriving, and each platform offers different ways for creators to connect with audiences and monetize their work. Whether you're building a brand or just sharing your passion, there's a platform (or two) waiting for you to take the plunge.

The Role of Social Media: The Backbone of the Creator Economy

Social media isn't just for selfies and vacation snaps anymore; it's the powerhouse behind the Creator Economy. In the old days (we're talking like 10 years ago), you needed a publishing deal, a record label, or a ton of luck to get your work seen by the masses. But thanks to social media, all you need is a phone and a Wi-Fi connection to broadcast your talents to the world. Here's how creators are leveraging social media to do just that.

Building an Audience:
Social media is where you find your people—the ones who care about what you create. Whether it's your thoughts on the latest Marvel movie or your tips on how to paint like a pro, social media helps you connect with like-minded folks. The beauty of it? There's a niche for *everything*. Seriously, even if your thing is teaching parrots how to ride skateboards, there's probably an audience for it.

Promoting Your Work:
Once you've found your tribe, social media helps you keep them engaged. Platforms like Instagram and TikTok are all about *real-time connection*. Creators post new content to show what they're working on, tease upcoming projects, or even get feedback on current work. It's like having a conversation with your audience, only instead of face-to-face, it's through a flurry of likes, comments, and shares.

Engagement is Key:
Here's a pro tip: It's not enough to just post and run. Creators who succeed in the social media game know that engagement is everything. Respond to comments, ask questions, create polls, and go live. The more you engage, the stronger your bond with your

audience—and the more loyal they'll become. Remember, people don't just follow creators for content; they follow for the connection.

Case Studies of Successful Creators: From Small Beginnings to Big Success

To give you a clearer picture of what's possible in the Creator Economy, let's look at a few real-life stories of creators who started small but have now built thriving careers.

Case Study 1: Emma Chamberlain (YouTube)
Emma started her YouTube channel as a teenager, filming vlogs in her bedroom with zero fancy equipment. Her quirky editing style and relatable humor quickly won over audiences, and before she knew it, she had millions of subscribers. Emma's authentic approach to content creation proved that you don't need a Hollywood budget to connect with people. She now has partnerships with luxury brands like Louis Vuitton and hosts a podcast with millions of listeners.

Case Study 2: Brittany Broski (TikTok)
Known for her viral "Kombucha Girl" video, Brittany turned a funny, off-the-cuff TikTok into a full-fledged career. She's now a comedian, content creator, and internet sensation, partnering with major brands and appearing on shows like *The Tonight Show*. Brittany's story is a testament to the power of going viral—but more importantly, to staying authentic and using that momentum to build a sustainable career.

Case Study 3: Marques Brownlee (YouTube)
Marques, also known as MKBHD, began his YouTube career reviewing tech gadgets. Starting with low-budget videos filmed in his bedroom, Marques consistently posted high-quality, informative content, building a reputation as one of the most trusted voices in tech. Fast forward to today: Marques has over 15 million subscribers and regularly collaborates with top tech brands like Apple and Google.

These case studies show that success in the Creator Economy doesn't come overnight, but it's certainly possible with consistency, authenticity, and a little bit of creativity. Whether you're starting with a smartphone and a dream or you've been creating for a while and need that extra push, these creators prove that the path to success is open to anyone willing to take the leap.

Chapter 2: Finding Your Niche in the Creator Economy

Welcome to the Niche Hunt: It's Like Shopping for Ideas, but Way More Fun

Let's think of your niche like a puzzle piece that's been missing all your life. It's a perfect fit between what you love and what the world wants. You'll feel that satisfying *click* when it all comes together. But here's the deal: finding your niche is crucial because, without it, you're just throwing spaghetti at the wall and hoping it sticks. And while spaghetti is delicious, it's not a great business strategy. You need focus, direction, and a clear spot in the creator ecosystem.

Step 1: Passion Meets Market Demand – The Sweet Spot

Why start with your passion? Because you're going to be spending a LOT of time creating content. You want to wake up excited about it, not dread it like a dentist appointment. And why add market demand to the mix? Because no matter how passionate you are about underwater basket weaving, if there's no audience, you're talking to yourself. And while self-talk is great, it won't pay the bills.

Breaking It Down:

- **Passion:** This keeps you energized and creative. If you don't enjoy what you're doing, that will come across, and you'll burn out faster than a candle at a rave.
- **Market Demand:** This is how you ensure there's an actual audience for what you're doing. Think of it as making sure the party you're throwing actually has guests—and snacks that they want to eat.

Example: You're super passionate about gaming, but you notice there's a huge untapped demand for "How to Play Retro Games Like a Pro." Now you've combined your love for gaming with something people are actively searching for. That's the sweet spot!

Step 2: Research the Competition – Because You Don't Want to Be a Copycat

Competition is everywhere. If you've got a great idea, chances are someone else has already thought of it too. But that's not a bad thing! It means there's interest in your niche, and you can use this to your advantage. Looking at your competition helps you figure out how to differentiate yourself. It's like showing up to a party wearing the same dress as someone else—totally fine, as long as you've got a killer accessory they didn't think of.

Why It Matters:
You don't want to blend in with the crowd. By researching the competition, you get a sense of who's doing what, and you can carve out your own space by doing something different or adding more value.

Example: Let's say you're a travel blogger. Everyone's already talking about budget travel and luxury travel, but hardly anyone is diving into "Sustainable Travel for Families." Now you're the cool kid with the fresh take!

Step 3: Test the Waters – Don't Commit Before You Try It On

Before you go all-in on your niche, it's smart to test it out. Think of this as dating before marriage. You wouldn't commit to a lifetime of content creation without knowing if it's really going to work for you, right? By testing your niche with free content, you get valuable feedback without the pressure of having to make it work from day one.

Why It's a Game-Changer:
It gives you insight into what works and what doesn't before you spend hours or dollars on something that flops. Testing gives you flexibility to pivot and improve before fully committing.

Example: You're thinking of starting a podcast about quirky inventions. Before investing in all the equipment, try out a few blog posts or YouTube videos on the topic. If people start saying, "I need more of this!" then you know you've struck gold. If you hear crickets, maybe tweak the idea.

Chapter 3: Building Your Personal Brand

Your Personal Brand: It's Your Superhero Identity, Minus the Cape (Unless Capes Are Your Thing)

Your brand is what people think of when they hear your name or see your content. It's like your personal flavor—whether that's spicy, sweet, or a mix of both. Your brand is *how* people connect with you and decide whether they want to stick around for the long haul. The cool thing? You get to create this identity and shape how people see you. So let's get started on making your brand unforgettable!

Step 1: Define Your "Why" – Your Brand's North Star

You might be thinking, "Why do I need to know my 'why'?" Well, here's the deal: Your 'why' is what keeps you going when things get tough. It's your driving force, and more importantly, it's what makes people care about what you're doing. If you're just in it for the money, people will sense that, and they won't stick around for long. But if you have a mission, a purpose behind what you're doing, that shines through.

Why It Matters:
People love to support creators with a purpose. When your audience knows *why* you're creating, they connect with you on a deeper level. Your "why" keeps you grounded, focused, and authentic.

Example: Imagine you're a fitness creator. Your 'why' might be to help people love their bodies without stressing about the number on the scale. Now every workout, post, or video you create ties back to that message. Your audience will know that you're not just another fitness influencer—you're *their* fitness guide.

Step 2: Consistency is King – Because People Need to Recognize You

Branding isn't just about logos and color schemes. It's about being consistent so people know what to expect from you. Think about your favorite show—would you keep watching if it suddenly changed tone or characters every episode? Of course not! Consistency builds trust. Your audience should be able to recognize your content whether they're scrolling through Instagram, YouTube, or TikTok.

Why It's Key:
Consistency builds familiarity, and familiarity builds trust. When people trust you, they'll keep coming back, share your content, and eventually become loyal fans (and customers!).

Example: Let's say you're a tech reviewer. If your tone is witty and sarcastic on Twitter, but serious and corporate on YouTube, people will be confused. Keep your voice and visuals consistent across platforms so people know they're getting the same awesome you no matter where they find you.

Step 3: Authenticity – No One Likes a Phony

In the creator economy, authenticity is your secret weapon. There's a reason why creators who are real about their struggles, flaws, and weird quirks tend to attract the most loyal audiences. People crave connection, and nothing kills connection faster than someone pretending to be something they're not. So don't try to be perfect—be you.

Why It Works:
People follow creators because they're real, not because they're polished and flawless. Authenticity breeds trust, and trust is everything

in the creator world. Plus, it's exhausting to pretend to be something you're not, so why bother?

Example: You're a DIY creator, and one of your projects turns into a hilarious disaster. Instead of pretending it never happened, share it with your audience. They'll love the behind-the-scenes look, and you'll become more relatable in their eyes. People love an "oops" moment—they've all been there.

Chapter 4: Monetizing Your Content

Monetizing: Time to Turn Those Likes Into Cash

You've built your audience, and now it's time to make some money. But here's the thing—making money in the creator economy isn't about being salesy or pushy. It's about offering value, being smart about partnerships, and diversifying your income streams so that if one thing falls through, you've got a backup plan. Think of it like planting multiple seeds in different gardens—if one doesn't grow, another one will.

Step 1: Ads and Sponsorships – Getting Paid to Promote What You Love

Why ads and sponsorships? Because companies love creators who have an engaged audience. They know that if your followers trust you, they're more likely to trust the brands you promote. But here's the golden rule: only promote products or services you genuinely love and believe in. Your audience can tell when you're faking it, and they won't hesitate to click "unfollow" if they feel like you're just a walking billboard.

Why It Works:
Sponsorships can be incredibly lucrative, and they're a win-win when done right. You get paid, and your audience gets introduced to products or services they might actually love.

Example: Let's say you're a beauty influencer, and a skincare brand offers you a sponsorship deal. If you've used and loved their products before, your promotion will feel authentic and valuable to your followers. But if you've never even heard of them, or worse, you don't like their products, promoting them will come across as inauthentic.

Chapter 5: Marketing Yourself

Marketing Yourself: Because Even Beyoncé Needs to Promote Her Albums

You might be thinking, "But I'm a creator, not a marketer!" Well, in the creator economy, you're both. Even if you have the best content in the world, if no one sees it, it might as well be buried in your grandma's attic. Marketing isn't just about shouting from the rooftops; it's about building connections, being strategic, and knowing where to put your energy. So, grab your megaphone (or just your phone), and let's get the word out about *you*.

Step 1: Utilizing Social Media Effectively – Your Free Billboard

Why social media? Because it's the digital equivalent of a crowded town square. Your audience is there, and it's where you can reach them directly. But here's the catch: not all platforms are created equal, and not all will work for you. The key is finding out where your audience hangs out and showing up consistently. It's like going to the cool kids' table at lunch—you need to be where the action is!

Why It's Crucial:
Different platforms serve different purposes. Instagram is great for visuals, YouTube is fantastic for long-form content, and TikTok? Well, that's where trends are born. Using the right platform in the right way

helps you maximize your reach and engage your audience in ways they already enjoy.

Example: If you're a photographer, Instagram is your playground. But if you're a DIY enthusiast who likes to explain projects step by step, YouTube might be your best friend. Know your strengths, and use the platform that amplifies them!

Step 2: Networking – Making Friends, Not Just Followers

Networking sounds stuffy, but it's really just a fancy word for building genuine connections. And in the creator economy, this is gold. Think of it like forming alliances in a video game—you help each other level up, fight off competition, and sometimes just have fun together. Whether you're collaborating with other creators, engaging with your audience, or connecting with brands, networking is about adding value and creating relationships that benefit everyone.

Why It Works:
Networking isn't just about what you get; it's about what you give. By being part of the creator community, you increase your visibility, gain support, and sometimes even find unexpected opportunities, like partnerships or guest spots on popular platforms.

Example: You're a food blogger, and you start engaging with a well-known nutritionist on social media. Before you know it, you're collaborating on a "Healthy Eating Challenge" that boosts both your profiles. Now you're being exposed to their audience, and they're being introduced to yours—a win-win!

Step 3: Content Marketing and SEO Basics – So Google Knows You Exist

Content marketing is essentially using your content to market yourself without sounding like a salesperson. It's subtle but powerful. And SEO? That's your secret weapon to get noticed in the sea of content. Think of SEO (Search Engine Optimization) as breadcrumbs you leave across the internet to lead people right to your digital doorstep. When done right, SEO makes sure that when people search for something you're an expert in, you pop up on the first page of Google (aka the Holy Grail of the internet).

Why It's a Big Deal:
If people can't find you, they can't follow you. SEO helps your content get discovered organically, without you having to constantly promote it. It's like laying the groundwork for your audience to come to you while you're busy creating more awesome stuff.

Example: Let's say you run a blog about sustainable fashion. By optimizing your posts with keywords like "eco-friendly clothing brands" or "how to build a sustainable wardrobe," you're increasing your chances of showing up when people search for those terms. And once they find you, they're hooked!

Chapter 6: Balancing Creativity and Business

Balancing Creativity and Business: Walking the Tightrope Without Falling Off

Being a creator sounds fun (and it is), but once you throw in the "business" side, it can start to feel like juggling chainsaws while riding a unicycle. One minute you're brainstorming brilliant content ideas, and the next you're staring at invoices wondering why no one warned you about the paperwork. The trick is finding that sweet spot where you can focus on your creativity without letting the business stuff drive you bananas.

Step 1: Time Management – When to Be Picasso, and When to Be the Accountant

Time management is your friend. Scratch that—it's your *lifesaver*. You might think you're going to spend all day creating, but the reality is there's a lot more to being a successful creator. You'll need time to manage emails, track expenses, negotiate partnerships, and still leave enough space to be, well, creative. Setting a schedule and sticking to it helps you keep your head above water.

Why It Matters:
Without time management, you'll find yourself overwhelmed and unproductive. It's like trying to herd cats—chaotic and impossible. But

when you structure your day, you free up mental space to focus on what matters: creating amazing content.

Example: Let's say you're an illustrator. You might set mornings aside for drawing and afternoons for answering emails, negotiating deals, and organizing your finances. By giving each task its own space, you keep everything running smoothly without sacrificing your creative flow.

Step 2: Avoiding Burnout – When Netflix Is a Must-Do

Let's be real—burnout is a sneaky villain in the creator world. It creeps up on you after weeks (or months) of non-stop creating, posting, and promoting. The key to avoiding it? Taking breaks. Yes, we're serious. Resting is just as important as hustling, and without it, you're going to hit a wall. Burnout not only zaps your creativity, but it can make you dread the very thing you once loved.

Why It's Essential:
You can't pour from an empty cup. Taking time to recharge ensures you're creating from a place of inspiration, not exhaustion. Plus, your audience can tell when you're not feeling it, and they'll tune out if your content starts feeling forced.

Example: After a few weeks of non-stop creating, you feel drained. Instead of pushing through, take a break. Go for a hike, binge-watch your favorite show, or spend a day offline. You'll come back with fresh ideas and renewed energy, and your content will be better for it.

Step 3: Setting Growth Goals – Because the Journey is Just as Important as the Destination

While it's fun to create for the sake of creating, setting goals helps you track your progress and stay motivated. These goals don't have to be massive—small wins are just as important. Maybe you want to reach a certain number of followers, land your first paid collaboration, or launch a new content series. Whatever it is, setting goals gives you something to work toward and celebrate when you achieve it!

Why It's a Game-Changer:
Goals give you direction and a sense of accomplishment. Without them, you're just floating through the creator world without a map. Plus, goals give you a reason to celebrate your progress, and we all need those little victories along the way.

Example: You set a goal to reach 5,000 followers by the end of the year. By focusing on this target, you create more engaging content, interact more with your audience, and even collaborate with other creators. When you hit that milestone, you celebrate (and maybe even do a little victory dance).

Chapter 7: Navigating Challenges in the Creator Economy

Challenges: The Bumps in the Road That Make You Stronger (Or Just Really Annoyed)

Alright, let's face it—being a creator isn't all filters and flawless selfies. There are some serious bumps in the road, and sometimes it feels like a rollercoaster you didn't sign up for. But, just like your grandma says, "What doesn't kill you makes you stronger." In this case, what doesn't kill your creativity can lead to a much stronger personal brand, some epic growth, and a few good stories for later.

But how do you deal with these bumps without losing your cool or burning out? Buckle up, because we're about to take you through some common challenges and how to tackle them with humor, grace, and maybe even a little eye-roll here and there.

Step 1: Handling Criticism – *Haters Gonna Hate, but You Don't Have To*

Let's be real—if you're putting yourself out there, **someone's gonna have something to say about it**. Whether it's constructive feedback or just someone having a bad day, you'll face criticism. The challenge is figuring out what to listen to and what to ignore. Here's the secret: not everyone's opinion matters.

Why It's Important:
If you treat every piece of criticism like a personal attack, you'll be stressed out 24/7 and second-guessing every decision. Learning to filter the good feedback from the noise is key to keeping your mental sanity intact and staying creative.

Example:
You post a funny, candid video, and someone comments, "This is cringe. Stop posting." Before you toss your camera out the window, take a breath. This person clearly doesn't get your humor, but you know your core audience does. Focus on the comments that celebrate your style, and ignore the rest. It's like when someone says they hate pizza. Clearly, their opinion can't be trusted.

Step 2: Dealing with Competition – *Yes, There's Room for Everyone*

One of the big, unspoken fears of the creator economy is competition. You might look around and think, "Everyone's already doing this. What's the point?" But here's the thing: **there's always room for you**. You bring your own unique flavor to the table, and that's what will set you apart.

Why It Works:
The creator economy thrives on individuality. Sure, there are a million travel bloggers, but only one *you* doing it in your way. The key is finding your voice and being confident in what makes you different.

Example:
Let's say you're starting a podcast about wellness, and there are already hundreds of similar ones. Instead of copying their format, you bring your quirky sense of humor and relatable struggles with meditation into the mix. Suddenly, you're not just another wellness podcaster—you're the *funny* wellness podcaster, and that's something people connect with.

Step 3: Legal Considerations – *Avoid the "Oops, That Was Illegal" Moment*

Ah, legal stuff—the least fun but most important challenge you'll face. From copyright issues to taxes, these are the grown-up problems we'd all rather avoid. But dodging them can lead to major headaches down the road, so it's better to tackle them early on.

Why It Matters:
The last thing you want is to build a successful brand, only to have it all crash down because of a copyright strike or a tax mishap. Taking care of the legal stuff means you're protecting your business and your content.

Example:
You're using a popular song in the background of your latest video. It's getting tons of views, but oops—you didn't have the rights to use that music. Suddenly, the video is taken down, and you're slapped with a warning. Lesson learned: always check for royalty-free music or get permission from the artist.

Chapter 8: How to Build a Creator Community

Building a Creator Community: Because It's Always Better to Share the Cake

You've heard the saying, "It takes a village." Well, it also takes a community to thrive as a creator. In the world of content creation, going solo might work for a while, but building a community can take you from good to legendary. Your community isn't just your audience; it's a group of people who support, promote, and genuinely engage with your content. Plus, it's way more fun when you have people cheering you on (and, let's be honest, liking your posts).

Step 1: Engaging With Your Audience – Be a Friend, Not a Broadcaster

Imagine you're at a party. Now, are you the person who talks non-stop about themselves and ignores everyone else? Hopefully not! Engaging with your audience is like hosting the best party—they should feel included and heard. Reply to comments, ask questions, and most importantly, *listen*. The more you interact, the more invested they'll be in your journey.

Why It Works:
People support creators they feel connected to. By making your audience feel like a part of your process, they're more likely to stick around, share your content, and root for you to succeed.

Example: You're a podcaster, and after each episode, you ask your listeners to send in their thoughts or questions. Not only does this give you more content ideas, but it also makes them feel involved. Plus, when you answer their questions on air, they'll feel like VIPs!

Step 2: Creating a Space for Your Community – Let's All Hang Out!

Your community needs a space to connect with you and each other. This could be a Facebook group, Discord server, or even a regular livestream. Think of it as a virtual hangout where everyone can share ideas, ask questions, and, most importantly, bond over their love for your content. The more active your community is, the more loyalty you'll build.

Why It's Important:
People love being part of something bigger than themselves. Creating a dedicated space for your community gives them a sense of belonging, which increases their connection to you. Plus, it's a great way to gather feedback, learn what your audience wants, and even spark collaboration ideas.

Example: You're a fitness influencer, and you start a Facebook group where your followers can share their progress, ask for advice, and post photos of their smoothie bowls (because, of course). Over time, the group becomes a mini-support network, and you're at the center of it all, with engaged, loyal fans who are more likely to stick with you for the long haul.

Step 3: Collaborating With Other Creators – Two (or More) Heads Are Better Than One

In the creator economy, collaboration isn't competition—it's expansion. When you team up with other creators, you're not only exposing your work to a new audience, but you're also giving your own fans something fresh and exciting. Plus, collaborations are a great way to learn from each other, boost creativity, and maybe even make a new friend.

Why It's a Power Move:
By collaborating with others, you get access to their audience, their expertise, and their creativity. It's like adding extra rocket fuel to your growth. Plus, it's fun! Who doesn't like working with cool people who "get it"?

Example: You're a travel vlogger, and you team up with a well-known photographer for a road trip series. While you're talking about places to visit, your photographer friend is sharing tips on how to capture the perfect sunset shot. Both audiences win, and so do you!

Chapter 9: How to Monetize as a Beginner (Without Feeling Like a Sellout)

Monetizing Your Content: Because We All Gotta Eat

Ah, monetization—the part where you actually start earning money for all your hard work. For some creators, this part can feel awkward. After all, you didn't start creating content just to make money, right? (Well, maybe a little.) The key to monetizing without feeling like a sellout is making sure the ways you earn income align with your brand and your values. You're not just cashing in—you're offering something valuable to your audience.

Step 1: Start Small – Every Penny Counts (And That's OK!)

Don't be discouraged if you're not making millions right out of the gate. Start small and build your income streams over time. Whether it's selling a few branded stickers or getting your first $10 from a Patreon supporter, small wins are still wins. The important thing is to lay the groundwork and grow from there.

Why It Works:
Starting small allows you to test the waters, learn what works, and build confidence. It also helps you avoid feeling overwhelmed by the pressure of making huge sums right away. Slow and steady, my friend.

Example: You've just launched a YouTube channel, and while you're not raking in ad revenue yet, you offer viewers the chance to support you on Patreon for $5 a month. A few fans sign up, and suddenly, you've got a monthly income that covers your coffee budget—progress!

Step 2: Diversify Your Income Streams – Because You Can't Live on Sponsorships Alone

Sponsorships are great, but they're not the only way to monetize. In fact, depending solely on one stream of income is risky. Think of your income streams like a buffet—you want a little bit of everything on your plate. So, in addition to sponsorships, consider affiliate marketing, selling products, offering services, or even creating paid content like e-courses.

Why It's Crucial:
When one income stream dries up (and it will at some point), having others in place keeps you afloat. Plus, different revenue sources tap into different parts of your audience—some will buy merch, while others might prefer to support you through donations.

Example: Let's say you're a beauty influencer. You've got a few sponsorships lined up, but you also create an affiliate link with your favorite skincare brand. When your audience buys through your link, you get a small commission. At the same time, you launch an e-book on DIY face masks, and voilà—three streams of income, one happy bank account.

Step 3: Set Boundaries – Not Every Dollar Is Worth It

As tempting as it is to take every sponsorship offer that comes your way, it's important to stay true to your brand. Your audience can smell inauthenticity from a mile away, and nothing loses trust faster than promoting products or services that don't align with your values. So, before you say yes to that deal, ask yourself: Is this something my audience will appreciate? Does it make sense for my brand?

Why It Matters:
Selling out might get you a quick paycheck, but it'll cost you in the long run. By only accepting deals that feel authentic, you're building a sustainable, trustworthy brand that your audience will stick with. And trust equals long-term income.

Example: You're a wellness blogger, and a fast-food chain offers you a big sponsorship deal. While the money is tempting, it doesn't align with your message of healthy living. Instead, you pass and wait for a brand that's a better fit, like an organic smoothie company. You'll keep your integrity—and your loyal audience.

Chapter 10: How to Stay Consistent Without Losing Your Mind

Staying Consistent: It's a Marathon, Not a Sprint (But There's Ice Cream at the End)

In the creator economy, **consistency is everything**. Whether you're posting videos, blogs, tweets, or TikToks, showing up regularly is what keeps your audience engaged and growing. But let's be honest: life happens. Sometimes, the thought of coming up with new content feels as appealing as running a marathon in flip-flops.

The trick is staying consistent *without losing your mind.* Luckily, we've got some tried-and-true strategies that will help you keep the momentum going and maybe even make it fun (yes, fun!).

Step 1: Create a Content Calendar – *Organization Is Sexy*

A content calendar is your best friend. It's like that super-organized friend who always knows what's happening and makes sure you don't double-book yourself. By planning out your content ahead of time, you avoid the "Oh no, I have to post something today!" panic.

Why It Works:
A content calendar keeps you on track, helps you plan for special

events or trending topics, and makes sure you're not repeating the same content over and over. Plus, it saves your sanity.

Example:
You're a fitness influencer, and you map out your content for the next month: Motivational Mondays, workout videos on Wednesdays, and food tips on Fridays. Now, instead of scrambling every day, you've got a clear game plan. More time for yoga, less time for stressing.

Step 2: Batch Content Creation – *Because One Shoot Is Better Than Ten*

Batching content means creating multiple pieces of content in one go. Instead of setting up your camera every single time you need a video, you film a bunch of them all at once. This saves you time, energy, and reduces the chances of those "I don't feel like filming" days getting in the way of your schedule.

Why It's Brilliant:
When you're already in the creative zone, it's easier to keep going than to start and stop constantly. Plus, you get ahead of the game, so if life throws a curveball (or you just need a break), you've still got content ready to go.

Example:
You're a food blogger, and instead of filming one recipe at a time, you dedicate one day to cooking and filming three recipes. Now you've got content for the next few weeks, and you only had to deal with the mess in your kitchen once.

Step 3: Automate Where You Can – *Robots to the Rescue*

In today's world, you don't have to do everything manually. There are tons of tools out there to help you automate parts of your content creation process. Scheduling posts, auto-responses, email newsletters—get the bots to do the boring stuff so you can focus on the creative part.

Why It Works:
Automation frees up your time for the things that really matter, like creating, connecting with your audience, and not having a meltdown trying to post at the exact right time every day.

Example:
You use a scheduling tool to plan out all your Instagram posts for the week in one sitting. Now, you can focus on interacting with your audience, knowing that your posts will go out like clockwork. It's like having an assistant, without the awkward small talk.

Chapter 11: How to Handle Criticism and Negative Feedback (Without Crying Into Your Pillow)

Dealing with Criticism: Haters Gonna Hate, But You're Gonna Create

No matter how amazing you are, criticism is inevitable in the creator economy. Whether it's a nasty comment on your latest post or a brutal review of your content, not everyone is going to be your biggest fan—and that's okay! The key is learning how to handle criticism without letting it derail your confidence (or send you into a spiral of overthinking and cookie-eating). Instead, let it fuel your growth.

Step 1: Don't Take It Personally – Sometimes, It's Really Not About You

It's easy to feel like criticism is a personal attack. Someone didn't like your video? Must mean they hate you, right? Wrong. Often, negative feedback says more about the critic than it does about you. Maybe they're having a bad day, or maybe your content wasn't for them—and that's fine. Your content won't resonate with *everyone*, and it's not supposed to.

Why It Works:
By not taking criticism personally, you create space to reflect on it rationally. Some feedback might be useful, and some might be pure nonsense. But you can't evaluate it properly if you're too caught up in your feelings.

Example: A follower leaves a scathing comment on your fitness vlog, saying, "This is the worst workout video I've ever seen." Ouch, right? Instead of spiraling, you calmly remind yourself that maybe this person just prefers a different style. You focus on the positive feedback you've received and keep doing your thing.

Step 2: Learn from Constructive Criticism – The Gold Hidden in the Dirt

Not all criticism is bad. Some of it can be genuinely helpful if you're willing to listen. Constructive criticism is like the vegetables of feedback—it might not taste great at first, but it'll make you stronger. When someone gives you well-meaning advice on how to improve, don't get defensive. Embrace it! It could be the very thing that helps you level up.

Why It's Powerful:
Constructive criticism gives you the opportunity to grow and improve. If someone's pointing out areas where you can get better, that's a gift, not a slap in the face. Every creator worth their salt has had to make adjustments and refine their work, and that's what makes them successful.

Example: A follower comments on your photography page, "I love your pictures, but some of them look a little over-edited." Instead of getting upset, you take the feedback to heart. You experiment with a more natural editing style, and soon enough, your audience loves the new look. Boom—growth!

Step 3: Let the Trolls Be Trolls – Don't Feed the Drama

Here's the thing: Trolls thrive on your reaction. They're not trying to help you improve; they're just there to stir the pot and get under your skin. The best way to deal with trolls is to ignore them. Don't engage, don't argue, and definitely don't lose sleep over their comments. You've got better things to do—like creating more awesome content!

Why It's Essential:
Engaging with trolls is a waste of time and energy. You'll never win an argument with someone who's just there to cause chaos. By refusing to engage, you're not giving them the satisfaction they crave, and you're protecting your peace.

Example: A troll leaves a nasty comment on your Instagram post, "This is the dumbest thing I've ever seen." Instead of clapping back or explaining yourself, you just shrug, smile, and keep scrolling. You've got bigger fish to fry (or tofu, if you're vegan).

Chapter 12: How to Stay Motivated When You Feel Like Giving Up

Staying Motivated: Sometimes You Gotta Be Your Own Cheerleader

Even the most passionate creators hit roadblocks where they feel like throwing in the towel. Maybe your content isn't gaining traction, or maybe you're just feeling burnt out. Whatever the case, staying motivated is key to long-term success in the creator economy. The good news? There are strategies to keep the fire burning, even on those days when you'd rather binge-watch Netflix than create.

Step 1: Remember Your 'Why' – Why Did You Start in the First Place?

When motivation starts to wane, it's time to reconnect with your 'why.' Why did you start creating in the first place? Was it to share your passion, inspire others, or build something meaningful? Write it down, and keep it somewhere visible. Whenever you're feeling discouraged, remind yourself of your purpose. It's easier to push through tough times when you're connected to your deeper reason for doing what you do.

Why It Works:
Your 'why' acts as your anchor. It's the thing that keeps you grounded

when things get tough. By staying focused on your bigger purpose, you can overcome temporary setbacks and keep moving forward.

Example: You're a mental health advocate, and you started your blog to help others overcome anxiety. Whenever you feel like giving up, you read the messages from readers who say your blog has changed their lives. Suddenly, your motivation returns—because it's not just about you; it's about them.

Step 2: Set Small, Achievable Goals – Because Tiny Wins Add Up

Feeling overwhelmed by the bigger picture? Break it down into smaller, bite-sized goals. Instead of focusing on hitting 100,000 subscribers, aim for 1,000 first. Then 5,000. Then 10,000. Celebrate each milestone along the way, because every step forward is progress—even if it's a baby step.

Why It's Motivating:
Big goals can feel daunting, but smaller goals are manageable. Each time you hit a small goal, you get a boost of motivation, which keeps you moving toward the next one. It's like leveling up in a video game—those little wins keep you hooked.

Example: You're a podcaster, and your goal is to land 10,000 listeners. Instead of fixating on that huge number, you set a goal to reach 500 listeners by the end of the month. When you hit it, you reward yourself with a (well-deserved) celebratory pizza.

Step 3: Take Breaks – Even Creators Need a Time-Out

Burnout is real, and trying to push through without taking breaks is a surefire way to hit a wall. Instead of constantly grinding, build rest into your routine. Whether it's taking a day off each week or scheduling mini-vacations, giving yourself time to recharge is crucial for staying motivated in the long run. (Yes, this is your permission to binge-watch Netflix guilt-free.)

Why It's Crucial:
Rest isn't a luxury—it's a necessity. When you give yourself time to rest, you come back to your work refreshed and full of new ideas. Plus, you avoid burning out, which means you can sustain your creative work over the long haul.

Example: You're a graphic designer, and after months of nonstop work, you're feeling drained. Instead of powering through, you take a weekend off to unplug and relax. By Monday, you're brimming with fresh ideas, and your motivation is back in full force.

Chapter 13: How to Keep Learning and Growing as a Creator

Continuous Learning: Because Even Masters Were Once Beginners

No matter how successful you become, there's always more to learn. The best creators are the ones who constantly push themselves to improve and adapt. Whether it's learning new skills, exploring new platforms, or staying up-to-date with industry trends, a commitment to continuous learning is what separates the good from the great.

Step 1: Stay Curious – Always Be Exploring

Curiosity is your best friend as a creator. Whether it's learning about a new editing software, trying a different content format, or exploring a new platform, staying curious keeps your work fresh and exciting. Plus, the more you learn, the more you can offer your audience.

Why It Works:
Curiosity keeps your content from becoming stale. By always looking for new ideas and ways to improve, you stay ahead of the curve and continue to evolve as a creator. Plus, learning is fun!

Example: You're a YouTuber who's always done traditional sit-down videos. One day, you decide to learn about live streaming and give it a try. Your audience loves the interactive format, and now you've got a whole new way to engage with them.

Step 2: Invest in Education – Whether It's Free or Paid

There's no shortage of resources out there to help you grow as a creator. From free YouTube tutorials to paid online courses, investing in your education is one of the best ways to level up your skills. It doesn't matter how much or how little you spend—the key is to keep learning and improving.

Why It's Important:
You're only as good as the tools in your toolkit. By continually learning and developing new skills, you stay competitive and ready to adapt to new challenges in the creator economy.

Example: You're a photographer, and you invest in an online course about advanced editing techniques. The course opens your eyes to new possibilities, and suddenly, your photos are getting more likes and shares than ever before. That investment? Totally worth it.

Step 3: Surround Yourself With Other Creators – Iron Sharpens Iron

One of the best ways to keep learning is by surrounding yourself with other creators. Whether it's through online forums, networking events, or just following other creators' work, being part of a community helps you stay inspired and motivated. Plus, you can learn a ton from other people's experiences and insights.

Why It Works:
When you're part of a community, you're constantly exposed to new ideas and perspectives. You can learn from others' successes (and failures) and apply those lessons to your own work.

Example: You join an online group of fellow creators, and through regular discussions, you learn about new tools, platforms, and strategies that you hadn't considered before. Your content gets better, and you've made some awesome friends in the process.

Conclusion: Go Forth and Create (And Don't Forget to Have Fun!)

Congratulations! You've made it through the wild world of the creator economy, from finding your niche and building your brand to mastering the art of monetization and dealing with trolls (with grace and a side of humor). You've learned how to stay motivated, handle criticism, and continually grow your skills. But here's the most important takeaway of all: **being a creator is an adventure**—one that's challenging, rewarding, and a whole lot of fun.

Remember, You're in Control of Your Own Story

The beauty of the creator economy is that you get to write your own narrative. You decide what kind of content to create, how to build your brand, and how to connect with your audience. And sure, it's not always going to be easy—there will be ups and downs, successes and setbacks. But the fact that you have the freedom to carve out your own path? That's pretty amazing.

Why It Matters:
When you embrace the creator's journey as your own, you'll be more resilient in the face of challenges. This isn't about fitting into a mold—it's about standing out as *you*. The creator economy thrives on authenticity, so never be afraid to let your true self shine.

Take It One Step at a Time

Don't feel like you need to have everything figured out right away. Growth takes time, and success doesn't happen overnight. The key is consistency. Keep creating, keep learning, and keep showing up. Your audience will find you, and your impact will grow. Take breaks when you need to, celebrate the small wins, and always be kind to yourself along the way.

Why It Works:
Small, consistent efforts over time lead to big results. It's the creators who stick with it, through thick and thin, who ultimately see the greatest success. Patience, persistence, and passion will take you further than you ever imagined.

You're Not Alone—The Creator Community Has Your Back

One of the coolest parts about being in the creator economy is that you're not flying solo. There's a whole community of creators out there, just like you, who are navigating the same challenges, learning the same lessons, and celebrating the same wins. Whether it's through online groups, collaborations, or mentorships, you'll always find people ready to support you on your journey. Don't hesitate to lean on them when you need a boost or some fresh ideas.

Why It's Powerful:
Community makes the journey more fun, more fulfilling, and more successful. By sharing your experiences and learning from others, you'll grow faster and enjoy the ride a whole lot more.

So, What's Next?

Now that you've got a solid foundation, the only thing left to do is *create*. Go ahead, take that first step—or that next step—and start building the creator empire you've always dreamed of. Whether you're vlogging, podcasting, designing, writing, or doing something totally out of the box, remember to stay true to yourself, stay curious, and above all—have fun.

The creator economy is waiting for you. Now go out there and show the world what you've got! 🎉

www.ingramcontent.com/pod-product-compliance
Lightning Source LLC
Chambersburg PA
CBHW070949220526
45471CB00007B/2957